Soft Skills and Professional Tips for the Office

Karen E. Mosier

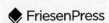 FriesenPress

Suite 300 - 990 Fort St
Victoria, BC, V8V 3K2
Canada

www.friesenpress.com

ISBN
978-1-5255-6733-9 (Hardcover)
978-1-5255-6734-6 (Paperback)
978-1-5255-6735-3 (eBook)

1. BUSINESS & ECONOMICS, BUSINESS COMMUNICATION

Distributed to the trade by The Ingram Book Company

To Dean – the joy of my heart

I would like to acknowledge my first boss *Dr. Raymond Tempier,* for having faith in my abilities, for giving me my first job, and for setting me on this exciting career path in Research Administration. I would also like to recognize my former boss *Dr. Baljit Singh,* who pushed me to stray outside my comfort zone so I could do so many things that I never dreamed it was possible for me to accomplish. Lastly, I would like to thank my current boss *Dr. Ivar Mendez,* for his support for my professional development, and for helping me truly understand the importance of respect and kindness in the workplace.

Special recognition to *Dr. Frances Chandler* for her guidance and mentorship to publish this book. Her extensive review of my manuscript and valuable comments and insights were greatly appreciated and contributed greatly to the quality of this published work.

PREAMBLE

In 2005, I started my first job as a Research Coordinator in the Department of Psychiatry at the University of Saskatchewan. When I began, research administration positions were increasing in number as the knowledge economy grew, but there were no training manuals or co-workers who could teach me the skills I needed to succeed in this field. Furthermore, as I soon found out, the job description did not include the myriad of skills I needed to effectively accomplish the tasks expected of me. I found myself learning on-the-fly; an inefficient method for both myself and my employer.

In my search for assistance, I found a plethora of books focusing on the hard skills employers were expecting of their employees but very few addressing the more elusive soft skills that are now acknowledged as being equally as important in today's workforce. As my career progressed and I learned more about the importance of learning and implementing these skills, I decided that I could assist others by documenting best practices in regards to working in an office setting.

The material presented in this book is a collection of my personal experiences and opinions on what has worked best for me based on trial and error, research, and the support of exemplary mentors. I acknowledge that my perception of the world is unique to me; predicated on my own ontology and personal experience. I also note that I have a generational bias, being in the latter part of my career, and that my examples are context specific.

Given these caveats, it is my belief that the content presented within this text will be useful to new, mid, and late career professionals who aspire to further develop their soft skills in an office setting.

Not all of the information contained in this manuscript will be new to readers, but I encourage those of you who do engage with this book, to embrace sections that are helpful to you and give less relevance to the rest.

Karen E. Mosier
December 15, 2019

Contents

INTRODUCTION

For new employees, starting a new job can be stressful. There is so much to learn and new people to meet. It takes a great deal of time to figure out who does what in the office, how everyone interacts, and what they are responsible for in this new role. Even after settling in, there are new people to meet, tasks to complete, and changes in policies and procedures that must be addressed. There are so many new skills that new employees need to acquire due to the changes in cultural norm. Some of these skills are not found in textbooks or courses and are considered to be intuitive such as how to develop good relationships with coworkers and managers, or how to communicate effectively with others.

For mid-career employees, it is easy to get comfortable in one's job. Routines and protocols are well known, and alliances and collaborations are established. There are always opportunities to learn more as effective employees, no matter where they are in their careers, to improve, modify, and self-reflect. Usually at this stage, they learn how to maintain a work-life balance and are making final decisions on where their careers are going.

Late-career employees look back and realize the years have flown by. As they enter the latter part of their careers, they self-reflect more often as they consider their accomplishments, failures, and potential legacies. They see their colleagues retire and new people enter the workforce. At this time in their careers, these employees think about taking on leadership roles, or not, and may wrestle with new technology, changing cultural norms and the new ideas that young people bring to the workplace.

The aforementioned examples highlight the changing face of work, the role and importance of *soft skills,* and the need to learn more even later in one's career. In the office, people with effective and appropriate soft skills are easy to identify, like Carol who can motivate most people to collaborate, to Marie who has an uncanny ability to work with even cantankerous people, to Dave who is the office listener, and voice of reason.

"Soft Skills and Professional Tips for the Office" is a great reference for office professionals. Easy to read and understand, it offers an excess of valuable advice to working men and women in an office environment. It provides real-life, applicable tips, for individuals who are in the early- to mid-stages of their careers and challenges later stage employees to step up and lead, in any capacity.

Although this book is not a document that would be distributed within offices, as it might be inappropriate for companies to dictate specific personal behavior, it is a useful tool for self-motivated individuals who seek advice on how to improve their performance on the job and in their personal lives as well.

PART 1:

NEW

EMPLOYEES

FIRST WEEK ON THE JOB

The first week is a stressful one for everyone including you, your new colleagues, supervisor, and employer. Be as prepared as you can to make the transition as smooth as possible. Before you start, find out who your main contact person is and inquire as to whether there are items that you need to bring or tasks that you need to perform prior to your arrival on the first day. Discuss what kind of training you can expect. Your first few days should be dedicated to getting you settled and determining the expectations of the position.

Get:

- A computer and other devices that your institution financially supports and allows you to possess

- A Photo ID, business cards, keys, door codes, a parking pass, and other personnel related forms and items

- Office supplies such as pens, pencils, erasers, paper, staplers, hole punches, staple remover, ruler, markers, name tags, etc.

- Someone to take you on a tour of the campus, building, parking facilities, washrooms, staff lounge, bookstore, and other relevant offices where people with whom you will interact are located

- All your personnel related forms completed regarding retirement, sick time, life insurance, dental and hospital care, eyeglasses and other aids, parental leave, tuition reimbursement, leaves of absence, payroll, next of kin, etc.

- A copy of your union agreement if applicable

- A copy of the organization chart with titles, names, and responsibilities attached to relevant people in the office

Determine:

- Where the office photocopier and printer are located and how to use them

- How you will secure your belongings such as your purse, phone, coat, boots, laptop, Ipad, lunch, etc.

- Expectations regarding flex hours, start and finish times, breaks, extra hours, (e.g., each week or during busy times only, lieu time or paid overtime?)

- Where the closest and/or most popular restaurants are located for coffee or quick lunches

- What union, if any, you may be required to join

- The range of learning opportunities open to you to enhance your skills

- Who you might be interested in engaging in a mentor/mentee capacity

- What the office and organizational norms are in regards to health and safety, working from home, coverage for holidays and other absences

- What benefits you qualify for and when they start

Set up:

- Your calendar, email, back up drive for files, relevant passwords, email signature, personal ID, systems for informing your supervisor and colleagues of any absences and mail delivery

- A time alone with your supervisor and individual coworkers

- A time to review all your rights and obligations with the relevant union and/or human resources personnel

- Opportunities to meet others outside of the office with whom you will interact

- Regular meeting times with your supervisor or others for at least the first few months

Additional Helpful Tips

Convey confidence: Arrive groomed, professionally dressed and with a positive attitude.

Practice professionalism: Carry a notebook and pen to write down instructions, advice, and other very important and relevant information pertaining to you, the job, your employer, and others with whom you will collaborate and interact.

Demonstrate diligence and dedication: Ask your supervisor what he/she thinks you should engage in to enhance your ability to do a good job. Be available by having your IT personnel set up remote access on your home computer and cell phone.

Be safe and secure: Ensure your workstation suits your physical capabilities and consider having someone complete an ergonomic review to make sure your monitors are set at the correct height, your keyboard is positioned correctly, and your chair is adjusted properly.

Attend to detail: It will take time to remember everyone's name so start by learning key names first and keeping a log of other names and items that remind you of them.

Listen and learn: Meet with individuals who you be charged with supporting. Listen to them, ask them what they need and deliver what you can in a timely manner. Outline your skills and credentials so as to instill their confidence in you. Let them know that their success is your success.

DEVELOPING A WORK PLAN

Get:

- Guidance from your boss as to your primary duties, e.g., plan research days, oversee research awards, organize resident luncheons, write annual research report

- Direction from your supervisor as to the type and date of research activities planned or ongoing. For example, are there designated research days, workshops, meet and greet events, networking lunches, or industry engagement dinners?

- A "stamp of approval" from your supervisor before you move forward on any project

Determine:

- What meeting(s) you are required to attend, what your role will be, and enter these dates into your schedule

- Where you can find the strategic plan of your institution and see how your unit fits into this plan

- If there is an existing budget for planned events related to your position and if not, develop one based on past norms

- The date of an event well in advance to give everyone involved at least 6 months' notice

- When public and religious celebrations take place and all statutory holidays and long weekends then refrain from planning events too close to these dates. Organize functions from September to June rather than in July and August when most people take vacation

- If your institution has any major events booked on the same date as your function involving the same constituents and be prepared to reschedule your activity

- The research interests of your faculty members so you can send them individual emails regarding relevant funding opportunities

- Which faculty members are applying to what funding opportunities so that you can send them reminders regarding internal reviews, institutional internal deadlines, funding agency deadlines, and remind them that you are available to review their grant prior to submission

Set Up:

- A 12-month timeline to include all proposed activities

- Meetings with individual and relevant researchers after you have learned about them from online sources. Be prepared with questions and appropriate supports you can provide to them when you meet

Additional Helpful Tips

Be Flexible: Accommodate unanticipated activities or events that may arise or tasks your supervisor suggests need attention.

Demonstrate Foresightedness: Apply for funding to help defray the cost of events, e.g., industry sponsors, education grants, workshop grants.

INTEROFFICE RELATIONSHIPS

Get:

- Information on the rules and/or culture of your workplace by talking to your supervisor and coworkers regarding expected working hours, ability to take holidays at certain times, etc.

- Acquainted with coworkers' allergies or sensitivities, e.g., Is your office a "no scent" or "peanut free" workplace? Does it have a "no high heels" policy? Are pets allowed?

Determine:

- How you can help around the office, e.g., add paper to photocopier, wash dishes in lunchroom, add a new water bottle on cooler, make a fresh pot of coffee, clean out the fridge, etc.

- Strategies to quell office gossip, e.g., evade, ignore, or make an outright statement about how you view gossip and what that term means to you

- Which people in your office are discreet, trustworthy, and/ or the best resource for challenges that you may experience

- How to keep interoffice banter to a minimum or where else you should converse so as not to disturb others

- What office social functions you are expected to attend or should attend to get to know your colleagues on a more personal level

Set Up:

- Activities to spend more time with your coworkers to get to know them better, e.g., go for lunch or a walk together, go to the gym after work or see a movie together, etc.

Additional Helpful Tips

Build Meaningful Relationships: Be friendly and take a few minutes each day for casual conversation, e.g., "Good Morning", "How was your weekend?", "How was the show?"

Demonstrate Objectivity: Formulate your own opinion on individuals you meet for the first time.

Express Appreciation: Thank people on a regular basis via email, a card, or small gift. Coworkers are more likely to assist people who show their appreciation.

Show Benevolence: Work together as a team and help each other to prevent mistakes. Accept responsibility, help others to find and fix errors, and give credit to others.

Practice Considerateness: Inform people in advance and as per office policies and accepted standards as to holidays you are taking. If you are ill, make sure to inform relevant coworkers by phone, email, or both.

Practice Professionalism: Speak politely at all times without profanity, remain calm in stressful situations and keep your emotions in check, and demonstrate a positive attitude. Use your coffee break or go for lunch if you want to share stories pertaining to your personal life with a coworker.

Model Respectful Behavior: Speak slowly and confidently in an appropriate voice tone, and convey positive, non-threatening nonverbal cues. Also be aware that personal space may vary by culture. Mentally limit your distance between yourself and your colleagues during conversations so that you do not unintentionally invade their personal space and make them feel uncomfortable.

COMMUNICATION STRATEGIES

Get:

- Information on who does what in your office. If you aren't sure if it is someone's job to do something, just ask them, e.g., "I need someone to do a travel expense claim for me. Is this your job or should I be asking someone else?"

Determine:

- Strategies, such as using a regularly updated group email list or have one designated person to send out office emails, to ensure inclusivity so that when information is sent out that everyone in the office is included, e.g., dates the boss is away on holidays, potluck lunch, date of the annual Christmas party, name and title of new employees, etc.

- To send important memos in advance to faculty & students & staff, e.g., dates when the department head/ADR/Dean is away & information regarding alternate replacements in their absence, date of research days/workshops, date of department/college retreats, etc.

Set Up:

- A big calendar in your office with a line for everyone with his or her name so that people can mark off when they are out of the office on business, on holidays or go home sick. This is extremely helpful for others to know so that if they need something, they know when people are around or are away and for how long

Additional Helpful Tips

Demonstrate Courtesy: If you cover a position with someone, be respectful and discuss this with your coworker ahead of time, if you have an appointment or are taking a day off or want to take vacation, so they are able to cover for you. It is also a good idea to let your colleagues know when you step out of the office and for how long in case someone is looking for you, or if you are expecting a package so that they can direct the person to your location. For office social events, plan things well in advance and do a doodle poll to get an idea of everyone's schedule and what date would work best for all to attend.

Respect Chain of Command: Know the chain of command and who reports to who and adhere to it to prevent negative feelings, e.g., talk to your supervisor first instead of talking to his/her boss directly.

Know Union Policies: Find out relevant information regarding employees to avoid interoffice conflict, e.g., supervising or being supervised by someone outside your union, differences in working hours between unions and/or contract employees, standardized hours versus flexible working hours.

Practice Good Listening Skills: For face-to-face communications, for clarity, repeat back to the individual a summary of what was discussed, and who will do what and by when.

EFFECTIVE MAIL
COMMUNICATION

Get:

- Informed on effective email communication through workshops, webinars, courses, books or other sources, e.g., proofread email 1-2 times for grammar or spelling before sending it, keep emails precise, bold any important item(s), send out all emails in lowercase only as using all caps can be interpreted as shouting and being rude, tone of email should be neutral or positive, use header to identify purpose of email for recipient

Determine:

- An effective strategy for email communications is to send out emails sparingly, e.g., know recipient's clinical or research interests and send targeted emails, be selective about what emails you send out to others, and reserve your emails for important matters such as a research day announcement or a weekly college newsletter

Set Up:

- A strategy to respond to a highly emotionally charged situation via email, e.g., take a break and clear your head and wait until you are calm before you respond, reread it more than once before you send it to check it for tone, keep tone of email neutral or positive, keep emotion out of the email, get a trusted colleague to review it prior to sending it

- A plan for when communications go awry, e.g., if you see a huge misunderstanding is occurring and multiple emails as a result, pick up the phone or go see the individual

Additional Helpful Tips

Show Foresight: If you go out of the office or on vacation set your out of office/vacation reply so that everyone knows that you are unavailable especially if the matter is urgent. Add the contact information for the person that can be contacted in your absence in your auto reply.

Practice Good Communication Skills: "Keep people in the loop" if you are working together with others, whether it is organizing a workshop, planning a meeting, or writing a group grant application, e.g., cc everyone involved on major emails related to the task, send out periodic email updates to everyone.

Practice Courtesy: Use "reply all" sparingly or preferably not at all as all recipients get unnecessary emails.

Exemplify Integrity: CC individuals on emails to another person rather than using bcc to be above board and transparent as to who is privy to the conversation.

Model Teamwork: CC other people on an email that need to know the information, e.g., food invoice or awards notification to your finance manager.

Prevent Email Tirades: For group emails always email yourself and then put your recipients into the blind carbon copy line. This can prevent potential embarrassment if one or more recipients hit reply all and a conversation goes back and forth, and everyone gets bombarded with dozens of emails.

REDUCING YOUR "NOISE" FOOTPRINT

Get:

- To know the rules of your workplace to know what is allowed and what is not allowed, e.g., radio is playing on office speakers, "soft heels only" policy, wear jeans on Fridays

Determine:

- How to be considerate to your coworkers and reduce your "noise" footprint, e.g., use your "inside" voice on the telephone, work quietly without talking out loud to yourself, make your personal calls during the lunch hour, eat your lunch in the lunchroom, chew gum outside regular working hours

- To be friendly to your colleagues and consider taking a few minutes to chit chat every day. Make the most of office social activities as an appropriate setting to get to know your colleagues and have time to talk and laugh and joke

Set Up:

- Your wardrobe accordingly to respect your coworkers and reduce office noise, e.g., If you find that your favourite bracelets clank on the chalkboard, keep them on your desk during working hours, and keep soft-walking shoes on hand if you find that your shoes create a distracting sound

- Your technologies to help limit unwanted noise in the office, e.g., set cell phone on vibrate, buy headphones to listen to music, keep your volume low on your headphones so others can't hear it, turn the volume off on your computer

- Alternate locations for meetings or conference calls to respect your coworkers' productivity

Additional Helpful Tips

Demonstrate Courtesy: If you need to answer your cell phone at work, step outside the door to answer it and keep walking until you can find a spot that won't disturb any adjacent offices.

NONVERBAL COMMUNICATION

Get:

- Informed on nonverbal communication and how people will subconsciously pick up on your behaviors without consciously thinking about it, e.g., crossed arms, frowning, touching your face, fidgeting, poor posture, hunching arms and shoulders together

Determine:

- To show your coworkers that you are approachable and friendly through your nonverbal communications, e.g., smile, interested facial expressions, good eye contact, etc.

- To demonstrate that you are interested in what others have to say through your nonverbal communications, e.g., good eye contact, shoulders lined up to face the speaker, leaning forward to listen to them, nodding in agreement, etc.

- To convey confidence through your nonverbal communications, e.g., smile, stand tall, strong stance, shoulders back, good posture, hands by your side, good eye contact, strong handshake, unmoving, looking forward, etc.

Set Up:

- A plan to monitor yourself so that your nonverbal communications align with your verbal communications, e.g., You say to your boss, "No problem I will do it right away" but you have a frown on your face, you say you like the idea at the meeting but you have your arms crossed the whole time, you say you are listening to your coworker but you keep looking at your cell phone or at the clock

Additional Helpful Tips

Show Professionalism: Read up on common office habits that can irritate others and monitor your own behavior and nonverbal gestures to demonstrate through your actions that you respect your coworkers. Always look people in the eye (where culturally appropriate) and give a strong handshake to project confidence and enthusiasm.

TIME MANAGEMENT

Get:

- Information and resources on time management, e.g., books, webinars, workshops

- Familiar with technology to assist you with time management, e.g., Outlook calendar and use it to keep track of everything that you need to remember, e.g., meetings, workshops, luncheons, grant deadlines, registration deadlines, birthdays, office socials, appointments. But more importantly, use it to remind yourself to do tasks, e.g., book food for lunch, send internal deadline reminder to faculty, send reminder to faculty to update webpages, book room for communications meeting, send out meeting agenda, send out final reminder for networking lunch, register for workshop

Decide:

- To monitor your working habits and do more difficult tasks during your peak performance hours and leave light, tedious tasks for periods of low performance, e.g., do filing or answer low priority emails the last 20 minutes of each day

Set Yourself Up:

- To develop a strategy to make the most of your time, e.g., Arrive 5-10 minutes early to unpack your stuff and be ready to start on time, grab your coffee before you start your shift or during your break, elude office talkers that can whittle your time away, add travel time into your schedule for meetings, add a time buffer in your schedule for meetings that regularly go overtime, give your regrets for meetings without a set agenda, focus on large tasks one at a time and do smaller stuff in between, always answer easy emails right away

Additional Helpful Tips

Listen and Learn: Take time to meet or go for coffee with experienced colleagues to ask what works best for them in terms of time management.

Demonstrate Punctuality: If you find that you arrive ~30 minutes late every day, reset your alarm and get up a half an hour earlier. Alternately, choose to get up a little earlier in the morning so that you don't have to feel rushed, and built a 15-minute buffer into your schedule so you are guaranteed to arrive on time. If you arrive early, use this time to put your things away, get your computer turned on, and/or grab a cup of coffee.

Show Respect: Be on time for every meeting because you value and respect your coworkers' time. Being on time will also keep the rest of your day on track.

Set Priorities: Keep your schedule open for the first hour of your workday. Use this time to determine and set your priorities for the day ahead. Be selective about the number of committees that you are on and about how many meetings that you need to attend.

Strive for Excellence: If you are finished a project, keep it and look it over one more time in the morning when you are feeling fresh and rested before you send it out.

Demonstrate Foresight: Purposely plan a lighter schedule during peak periods to compensate for greater workloads due to the time sensitive nature of pending deadlines.

Practice Healthy Habits: Take regular breaks and stand up or move around at least once every hour. Use your lunch break to step away from your desk and have lunch with a colleague or go for a walk outside. If you get so busy during peak times that you can't take breaks, try to build some exercise into your routine, e.g., walk to a washroom that is further away from your office, walk over to the general office to do some printing.

BULLYING

Get:

- Educated about bullying in the workplace through workshops, classes, books, webinars, and online sources, e.g., repeated behavior for many months or years where one individual tries to dominate or intimidate another person

Determine:

- If there is a zero-tolerance policy regarding bullying in your workplace and ask for office wide training to combat this problem

- To report the problem if you are being bullied. Victims of bullying may be hesitant to report the problem as they may think it could negatively affect their reputation and/or no one will believe them

- If other colleagues have had trouble with this individual. Talk discreetly to others in your office to find out if they have been bullied

Set Up:

- A plan to respond to bullying if it should occur or to help a colleague that is being bullied, e.g., first start by talking to the person that is bullying you and tell him/her how uncomfortable it makes you feel and ask him/her to stop, if this doesn't work, talk to your supervisor and explain the situation and if nothing is done talk to HR

Additional Helpful Tips

Demonstrate Resiliency: If you are constantly bullied, and management hasn't taken steps to fix the problem in a timely manner, find yourself another job with a more positive environment to work in, e.g., update your resume, check the job sites daily, check around with colleagues about upcoming job openings, take training to update your skill set, etc.

Practice Self Care: If you are biding your time working in a negative environment until you can find a different job, there are many strategies that you can employ to protect yourself until you can give your notice, e.g., take assertiveness classes, take your breaks & lunch hour at separate times and book your vacations on separate dates, try to minimize the time that you work together on joint projects, take up a new hobby or class to keep your mind off the bad environment at work, practice meditation, seek social support, write down your feelings to release your pent up emotions, practice daily exercise to get rid of feelings of frustration and anger, e.g., exercise bike, aquacise, weights.

REBRANDING FAILURE

Get:

- Information and resources on how to deal with failure in the workplace, e.g., everyone makes mistakes, to make a mistake is human, unrealistic expectations if a boss expects a perfect job every time, move outside your comfort zone and learn from your mistakes, see mistakes as a learning opportunity

Determine:

- To reflect on your failures and make safeguards to reduce repeated errors, e.g., make notes of what worked and what didn't work, put reminders in your calendar for next year, plan to start the task earlier next year, get more help for the next event, etc.

Set Up:

- A plan to pay attention to factors that can contribute to increased error rates, e.g., stress, pending deadlines, too much to do, doing too many things at one time, not taking breaks, not getting enough sleep, not eating right

- A strategy to see if you can make any small changes to reduce your error rate, e.g., keep on top of tasks to get them out of the way and always be planning ahead to get as many things done in advance, organize your schedule lighter around peak deadlines, try to focus on one task at a time, take your breaks and lunch hour, practice stress reduction techniques, do regular exercise, get enough sleep, eat right to nourish your brain

Additional Helpful Tips

Demonstrate Accountability: If you make a mistake, own up, and apologize. Take full responsibility for your actions. People will respect you for it.

Demonstrate Openness to Feedback: Remember that no improvement can be made without critique. Be open to take any negative comments from your supervisor/colleagues as an opportunity for improvement and consider what type of training you could take to improve your skills in these areas.

Share Your Wisdom: Use the knowledge that you have learned from your experience and organize a lunch and learn or present at a conference and teach others what you have learned by going through an experience (e.g., facilitating a large international grant application) and talk about what worked and what mistakes you made along the way.

PART 2:

MID-CAREER

EMPLOYEES

HOW TO DEVELOP RELATIONSHIPS WITH YOUR FACULTY

Get:

- To know your faculty. Remember your engagement with a faculty member will always be anywhere from zero to 100%. Persevere even if he or she doesn't want to work with you. Keep in mind the experience and years of service of the faculty member. A faculty member that has had huge success and has brought in thousands of dollars in research funding may not need any help or a faculty member that is close to retirement or has achieved tenure might not have the same goals as a new hired faculty member

Determine:

- Your niche and where you fit in the organization. If you start a new job it may take a year or two for faculty to get to know you so stay encouraged in the meantime

- To find the keeners among your faculty that are motivated and are passionate about doing research and work with them. Usually new faculty are good to approach as it usually part of their hiring package that they need to do research and they will need funding & papers for purposes of promotion & tenure

Set Up:

- A strategy to establish trust with your faculty. You will have to start small and show them that you are there to help them save time, e.g., provide RSEO contact information, send them available funding opportunities, liaison with the ethics office to get them the right ethics application, send them examples of successful grant applications, etc. Eventually they will realize that you are a good resource and start to work with you more

Additional Helpful Tips

Take Initiative: A good strategy to develop a strong relationship with a faculty member (instead of bombarding them with generic emails) is to send them personalized emails of specific funding opportunities that are relevant to their own area of research.

Be Proactive: Be proactive and send your faculty member a list of applicable funding opportunities suitable to their area of research in chronical order sorted by the deadlines with a working link to each funding agency listed within the document.

Be Strategic: Be a connector for your faculty, and when an opportunity presents itself, facilitate connections with your faculty with other researchers outside your unit or college. Organize "themed" networking lunches for your faculty and invite researchers from other departments/colleges to present their research & explore collaborative opportunities.

Highlight Your Faculty's Accomplishments: Have a bi-weekly communique or monthly newsletter to feature your faculty's achievements. Take the time to give personal congratulations to your faculty on their accomplishments, either verbally or via email.

PROFESSIONAL DEVELOPMENT

Get:

- Informed as to whether your company gives a yearly allotment to its employees for professional development and how much it is

- Knowledgeable about any training available through your organization or through other sources and take advantage of it, e.g., MS Excel, Access, SharePoint, InDesign

- Creative and check out free resources available on the internet or free online courses, classes and tutorials to upgrade your skill set, e.g., Canvas Network or Lynda.com

Decide:

- To take any courses or certifications related to your position. Training will strengthen your resume and show your employer that you are eager to improve your skill set

- To check for professional associations depending on your type of job such as CARA, CAUBO or ARMA that offer professional development and take advantage of these resources, e.g., participate in conferences, workshops, webinars, certification programs, etc.

Set Up:

- A strategy to be where you would like to be in terms of your career 5-10 years down the road. If there is a specific job that you would like to advance into what are the qualifications needed to apply for this job and if it is a certificate or program, plan how you will find the time around your work schedule to get it completed in the required length of time, e.g., Charted Professional Accountant, Masters in Business Administration, Certificate in Research Administration, Certificate in Research Management

- A plan to promote professional development in your workplace. Share information that may be useful to your colleagues through email networks. Forward professional development opportunities to your coworkers (e.g., conferences, workshops, webinars, classes) and facilitate information sessions that they can attend, e.g., CARA webinars, Brown Bag Lunches, Research Facilitator Lunch & Learn, etc.

Additional Helpful Tips

Demonstrate Perseverance: Prioritize your time to take training. Be diligent and get your courses done and out of the way. Also, with age, it can be harder to learn new things compared to having just come out of high school.

Find a Mentor: If you ever have an opportunity to get a mentor, I would strongly advise you to take it. A mentor can help you brainstorm how you want your career to progress. A mentor can give insight from their own work experience and guide you how to move forward with your goals to get where you want to be. Many individuals may be too busy or reluctant to commit to a formal mentor-mentee relationship, but even informal mentors can make a big difference to your career with their valuable advice.

Seek Wise Counsel: There are tons of courses and workshops available and they would all gladly take your money. If you aren't sure which ones to take, I find it helpful to ask my colleagues if they have taken any courses and specifically, which ones they really liked. Alternatively, I use the direct approach and mention the name of the course or workshop and ask around and see what everyone thought of it, what they learned, and if it was worth the money to take it.

THE POWER OF BREAKING BREAD

Get:

- Informed about the power of breaking bread and strategies to develop good relationships with your coworkers, e.g., books, workshops, courses, online sources, etc.

Determine:

- How to take advantage of and participate in office get-togethers as a fun and easy way to get to know each other and build meaningful relationships, e.g., potluck luncheons, birthday parties, annual Christmas party

- To be strategic and organize functions to promote appreciation for employees in your unit/organization, e.g., National Administrator's day, Teacher Awards banquet, Tri-Agency Award Winners luncheon, RSEO Appreciation event

- To be intentional and facilitate events to support networking and collaborations, e.g., Networking lunches, Meet Our Faculty luncheons

- To be tactical and arrange activities to facilitate educational opportunities, e.g., Resident Informational luncheons, research workshops, Research Rounds

Set Up:

- A plan to create a community of practice for people with similar duties to yours to meet and have lunch every few months and exchange ideas and best practices and network

Additional Helpful Tips

Seek Advice: Going out for coffee with a colleague can lead to a lasting friendship or be the start of an informal mentor/ mentee relationship.

Promote Relationships: If you want to be the most popular person in your office, keep a replenished bowl of mini chocolate bars at your desk for anyone to stop by and grab one. It is a quick and easy way to get to know everyone.

Spread Kindness: To cheer up a coworker, surprise them by buying them a coffee and/or a muffin. To dampen those winter blues, bring a fresh loaf of banana bread for your colleagues. Summer is a good time to organize a lunch and get everyone out of the office so they can to know each other better in a non-work setting. Bringing baked goods to the office can boost office moral (and your popularity). To show appreciation for your audio- visual support personnel you could buy them a dozen muffins and bring it to their office for them to enjoy.

Organize a Social Fund: Organize a social fund and have everything chip in money. Use it to celebrate birthdays, and buy a cake every month, and celebrate whoever has a birthday that month together. This will make everyone in your office feel appreciated and this social event will give everyone a chance to step away from their desk and talk with each other.

WORK LIFE BALANCE

Get:

- Information and resources on work life balance, e.g., books, webinars, workshops, internet, etc.

Determine:

- To take your job less seriously and have a life outside of work, e.g., social activities, exercise, sports, hobbies, etc.

- To put your health above your job, e.g., prioritize all doctor's appointments, eat right, exercise and get enough sleep no matter how busy you are

Set Up:

- A plan to implement healthy practices at work and to maintain balance between work and your home life, e.g., take regular breaks, use your lunch hour to get away from the office, take all of your vacation time, exercise, eat right, get enough sleep, have hobbies that you enjoy, regularly visit with family and friends

Additional Helpful Tips

Demonstrate Creativity: If your busy agenda doesn't permit time to exercise, schedule exercise into your daily routine, e.g., do yoga in your office over the lunch hour, walk or bike to work every day, download a stretch break app on your computer, do a staircase circuit workout, etc.

Use De-Stressing Strategies: If you have periods where you work longer hours (e.g., pending grant deadline, all day workshop & awards dinner) schedule time off in lieu of overtime as soon as possible so you can gear down and de-stress and get some rest.

Seek Solace: Always try to leave your office to eat your lunch. Getting away from your desk and your phone will make a world of difference. Connect with nature by going outside and going for a walk over the lunch hour. Life can get busy and chaotic at times and it may feel like everything is just going too fast. In moments like these, deliberately slow things down by taking time to regain your perspective, e.g., go for a walk, grab tea and a biscuit, go for lunch with a friend, etc.

Reward Yourself: Hard work isn't always recognized or rewarded. Always remember to reward yourself for doing a good job. Give yourself a pat on the back for a job well done. For big accomplishments, tell yourself in advance that once this is over you will reward yourself with something nice, e.g., foot massage, chocolate cupcakes, movie, tickets to the basketball game, etc.

Prioritize Your Schedule: Spend time with your family and friends and purposely schedule time in your calendar to make it happen. These interactions will help remind you that there is a lot more to life than just working all the time.

Combat Negativity: When things go wrong in the workplace, refocus your own energy by finding ways to do nice things for other people.

Help Others: Consider being a volunteer. Meeting different people and working with people less fortunate than yourself is a great way to keep your perspective and appreciate all that you have.

JOB ADVANCEMENT

Get:

- Knowledgeable about the job opportunities at your organization and determine what types of jobs that you could qualify for with your current skill set and experience and what type of training you would need to be considered for a job promotion, e.g., check job descriptions on company website, talk to other colleagues about their job descriptions, training and background, and career trajectory

Determine:

- To bloom where you are planted until you are promoted. Remember that your supervisor/colleagues may be asked about your work habits by your new potential employer or be asked for a letter of reference

- To persevere if you don't really like your current job or job environment. Remember that you won't have to do this job for the rest of your life so see it as a learning opportunity to develop your skill set and a stepping-stone to your next position

- To be persistent and understand that that you won't always get every job that you apply for, no matter how good your qualifications are and how much experience you have, because there are other factors involved, e.g., internal hiring, faculty spousal hires, nepotism, organizational prerogative to only hire employees at the bottom of the pay scale. If you didn't get the job that you really wanted, keep hope that a different job will come along and you will be offered the position

Set Up:

- A plan based on where you would like to see yourself in 5 – 10 years and take the necessary steps to obtain the education that you need so you are qualified to apply for the type of job that you really want, e.g., Masters in Business Administration, Charted Professional Accountant, Masters in Public Policy, Certificate in Research Administration, Certificate in Research Management, etc.

Additional Helpful Tips

Show Your Willingness to Learn: Let your boss know that you are willing to take training to improve your skill set.

Demonstrate Diligence: Work hard at what you do and eventually someone will notice how hard you are working. Establishing a reputation as an employee with a strong work ethic will give you a distinct advantage when you go for your job interview.

Be Realistic: Realize that your career won't always follow a linear fashion. You can't always just work your way to the top of your organization. Keep hopeful and watch for unanticipated positions that come up. Opportunities come around only occasionally, but they usually don't last for long. If someone offers you a really great job, make your decision carefully and quickly. Grab it before the opportunity is gone.

Think Beyond The Money: Think of your health above how much money you make. If your current job has very high levels of stress, but a different job has less stress but it pays less, you might want to consider the latter option in terms of your long-term health. Also, if you take a job that pays better, but your coworkers and/or boss aren't very nice, they can make your life a living hell.

Strive To Be Happy: Remain positive even if you are passed up for new job opportunities. Your coworkers and/or bosses may change jobs and if their organization is looking for new employees, they may think of you and your happy disposition and you could be offered a job to work there too. In this day and age, employers are looking more and more for employees that are pleasant and easy to work with.

Seek Job Satisfaction: The people that you work with are key to your job satisfaction. If you love your job and the people you work with, you don't have to change jobs or climb up the career ladder if you are perfectly happy where you are.

PART 3:

LATE-CAREER

EMPLOYEES

BE A LEADER

Get:

- Knowledgeable about what it takes to be a leader through courses, books, online sources, Ted talks, etc., e.g., everyone can be a leader whether or not they have a management position, if you have practical skills that can help someone else you need to step up as a leader, as a leader you can get to know people, inspire people and impact other's lives for good

Determine:

- To step up and be a leader in your office and help others in your workplace that could benefit from your knowledge and experience, e.g., help newly hired individuals that may be overwhelmed with all the information that they need to learn, be the one person in your office that everyone comes to ask for help

- To demonstrate initiative and seek out a leadership role to benefit your organization and give you an opportunity to get involved with something that you really care about, e.g., chairing the Communications committee, serving on your union's bargaining team, putting your name forward to be on your union's executive committee, leading the organizing committee for a conference

Set Up:

- A plan to mentor others. Mentoring doesn't cost anything but your time, and it can be very rewarding. Be strategic and commit yourself to mentor at least one person per year. This mentee could be from your office or from a different organization. If possible, make time to meet with them face-to-face for lunch once a month. As the years progress, you can step back and watch their careers blossom and be happy knowing that you had a small part to play in their success

Additional Helpful Tips

Don't Overcomplicate Leadership: True leadership can be as subtle as making new employees feel welcome to introducing them around the office to showing them how to use the photocopier.

Help Others To Lead: Looking for a simple way to be a leader in your workplace? For example, if you have been the Chair of the social committee for the last 5 years, you would be in an ideal position to guide the incumbent to take on this new role.

Reap Benefits of Being a Leader: Did you know that being a leader has great benefits for you too? Through helping others, you can improve your communication skills, develop negotiation skills, gain management skills, hone your problem-solving skills, and improve your resume, just to name a few benefits.

SPREAD SOME KINDNESS

Get:

- Knowledgeable about the power of kindness through classes, books, online courses, or other sources, e.g., a kind deed can change our mood completely, random acts of kindness leave a lasting impression with the recipient, kindness is an effective tool to combat negativity in the workplace to flip negative energy into positive energy

Determine:

- To improve your relationships with your coworkers and raise the morale in your workplace by carrying out random acts of kindness, e.g., opening the door for someone, giving someone praise "great job on the presentation", making a fresh pot of coffee, cleaning the microwave in the lunchroom, etc.

Set Up:

- A plan to launch a kindness campaign in your office and/or organization. Watch out for opportunities where you can do random act of kindness for others, e.g., it's fiscal year end so buy your Finance Manager a cup of coffee and a muffin, there is difficulty launching a new campus wide software program so walk over 2 dozen doughnuts for your IT people, you are working together with a colleague on a large project so you buy her an inexpensive oil diffuser that she has always wanted

Additional Helpful Tips

Demonstrate Appreciation: Buy thank you cards for your colleagues for their help on a large project or group activity and write out inspiring quotes or kind words to show your appreciation. Alternatively, make a list of people that have really helped you throughout the year and send out hand signed Christmas cards to acknowledge your thanks for their assistance.

Be Inclusive: Say good morning to everyone in the office so that no one feels left out and take the time to find out the names of everyone on your floor and greet them by name.

Nominate Colleagues for Awards: A great way to spread some kindness campaign at a whole new level is to nominate colleagues in your office/institution or outside your institution for awards, e.g., Staff Excellence Award, Spirit of the College Award, CARA Award, etc. Make it your goal to nominate at least one person per year for an award.

YOUR LEGACY

Get:

- Knowledgeable about leaving a great legacy or your mark on this world through workshops, classes, books, online sources, etc.

Determine:

- To reflect on what others might think of you after you retire and what you have accomplished during your career? Think of your own office and any past jobs that you have had, there are always a couple of people that stand out in every office, that make it a better place to work in just by their efforts and their attitude. Are you one of these people?

- To surround yourself with and get to know people that are inspiring and uplifting to motivate you to see what you can do to change other peoples' lives for good. Remember passion is contagious but so is complacency

Set Up:

- A plan to come up with ideas to be an agent of change and decide what you could do to change your organization for the better. Talk about your thoughts for your legacy with family, friends or trusted colleagues and formulate a concrete plan

Additional Helpful Tips

Start Small: A legacy doesn't have to be big. It can be what you want it to be, e.g., I want to be known as the "go to" person in my office, I want to be known as the cheeriest person in my office, I want to be known as the kindest person in the office.

Do What You Can: You don't have to be wealthy to leave a legacy or mark on other people's lives, e.g., donate $500 for a student award or staff appreciation award in your unit, earmark your pension after your death to establish a student scholarship, donate money for CARA bursaries.

Mentor Others: A good way to establish your legacy as you move through your career is to mentor other colleagues and then watch as their careers blossom knowing you had a small part to play in making this happen. Mentoring others can be very rewarding.

Keep It Simple: A legacy can be as simple as being a champion and spearheading something that hasn't been done before in your unit/department/college (e.g., pocket-sized orientation handbook for new residents, online resident research course).

Inspire Others: Motivate others by your actions to do great things themselves, e.g., write a book on Research Administration, implement a CARA volunteer recognition program, write member profiles for your union newsletter.

Let Your Actions Speak for You: Many people leave a legacy, but they don't realize it. Many "unsung heroes" in the office that are dedicated, always show up early for office functions, that help organize everything and tirelessly clean everything up, and then stand quietly in the back of the room while some other person generally takes all the credit. These people have left their "legacy" without saying a word. Remember actions talk louder than words.

 **Karen E. Mosier** has a BA (Honors) in Psychology and a MSc in Pharmacy. She has 14 years' experience working in research administration at the University of Saskatchewan. Karen has been a member of the Canadian Association of Research Administrators (CARA) since 2010 and has received two CARA awards: the Dan Chase Distinguished Service Award – Priority Initiatives in 2018 and the Community Builder Award in 2019. She is actively involved with CARA's Certificate in Research Administration program mentoring colleagues from across Canada and has served on the Research Administration Certification Program (Mohawk College) Advisory Committee since 2018. Karen lives in Saskatoon, Saskatchewan with her partner Dean.

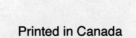
Printed in Canada